Viktoria Schoja

Determining Consumer Behaviour in the Catering Industry

A Case Study Of Starbucks UK

Anchor Academic
Publishing

Schoja, Viktoria: Determining Consumer Behaviour in the Catering Industry. A Case Study Of Starbucks UK, Hamburg, Anchor Academic Publishing 2016

Buch-ISBN: 978-3-96067-022-3
PDF-eBook-ISBN: 978-3-96067-522-8
Druck/Herstellung: Anchor Academic Publishing, Hamburg, 2016

Bibliografische Information der Deutschen Nationalbibliothek:
Die Deutsche Nationalbibliothek verzeichnet diese Publikation in der Deutschen Nationalbibliografie; detaillierte bibliografische Daten sind im Internet über http://dnb.d-nb.de abrufbar.

Bibliographical Information of the German National Library:
The German National Library lists this publication in the German National Bibliography. Detailed bibliographic data can be found at: http://dnb.d-nb.de

All rights reserved. This publication may not be reproduced, stored in a retrieval system or transmitted, in any form or by any means, electronic, mechanical, photocopying, recording or otherwise, without the prior permission of the publishers.

Das Werk einschließlich aller seiner Teile ist urheberrechtlich geschützt. Jede Verwertung außerhalb der Grenzen des Urheberrechtsgesetzes ist ohne Zustimmung des Verlages unzulässig und strafbar. Dies gilt insbesondere für Vervielfältigungen, Übersetzungen, Mikroverfilmungen und die Einspeicherung und Bearbeitung in elektronischen Systemen.

Die Wiedergabe von Gebrauchsnamen, Handelsnamen, Warenbezeichnungen usw. in diesem Werk berechtigt auch ohne besondere Kennzeichnung nicht zu der Annahme, dass solche Namen im Sinne der Warenzeichen- und Markenschutz-Gesetzgebung als frei zu betrachten wären und daher von jedermann benutzt werden dürften.

Die Informationen in diesem Werk wurden mit Sorgfalt erarbeitet. Dennoch können Fehler nicht vollständig ausgeschlossen werden und die Diplomica Verlag GmbH, die Autoren oder Übersetzer übernehmen keine juristische Verantwortung oder irgendeine Haftung für evtl. verbliebene fehlerhafte Angaben und deren Folgen.

Alle Rechte vorbehalten

© Anchor Academic Publishing, Imprint der Diplomica Verlag GmbH
Hermannstal 119k, 22119 Hamburg
http://www.diplomica-verlag.de, Hamburg 2016
Printed in Germany

Acknowledgements

I would like to express my gratitude to my supervisor Dr. Svetla Stoyanova, who supported and encouraged me during this research, to Student Services and the Learning Resources Centre at the Coventry University, London Campus, especially to David Brown for the advice and support.

Table of Contents

Acknowledgements 1
Table of figures 4
Abstract 5
1. Introduction 6
   1.1 The Purpose of this Research 6
   1.2 Structure of this Research 6
   1.2 Research Questions 6
   1.3 Research Objectives 7
   1.4 Company Background 7
2. Literature Review 9
   2.1 Overview 9
   2.2 Relevant Literature 9
      2.2.1 Customer Satisfaction and Dissatisfaction 9
      2.2.2 Customer's Expectation 10
      2.2.3 Customer's Perception 10
      2.2.4 Consumer Behaviour Influences 11
      2.2.5 Consumer Decision Making 11
      2.2.6 Previous Research on Consumer Behaviour within the Catering Industry 12
      2.2.7 Service Quality 13
      2.2.8 Conceptual Framework 13
   2.3 Conclusion of the Literature Review 15
3. Research Methodology 16
   3.1 Overview 16
   3.2 Research Process 17
   3.2 Research Design 17
      3.2.1 Research Philosophy 17
      3.2.2 Research Approaches 18
      3.2.3 Types of Studies 19
      3.2.4 Research Strategies 19
      3.2.5 Time Horizons 20
      3.2.6 Techniques and Procedures 21
   3.3 Primary Data Collection Process 21
      3.3.1 Sampling 22

- 3.4 Validity 23
- 3.5 Reliability 23
- 3.6 Generalizability 23
- 3.7 Ethical Issues 23
- 3.6 Limitations 24
- 4. Results 25
  - 4.1 Pilot Test Findings 25
    - 4.1.1 Negative Critique, Question 5 25
    - 4.1.2 Negative Critique, Questions 6-8 25
    - 4.1.3 Positive Critique 26
  - 4.2 Findings, Interpretation and Discussion 27
    - 4.2.1 General - Questions 1-3 27
    - 4.2.2 Consumer Behaviour Service Quality - Question 4 29
    - 4.2.3 Consumer Behaviour Decision Making - Question 5 30
    - 4.2.4. Consumer Behaviour Taxes – Question 5 32
    - 4.2.4 Starbucks - Questions 6-9 33
    - 4.2.5 Association – Question 9 36
- 5. Conclusion 37
  - 5.1 Conclusion for the Researcher 38
- 6. Recommendations 38
- References 39
- Appendices 41
  - Appendix 1 - Questionnaire for the primary research 41
  - Appendix 2 - Findings from the primary research 44
  - Appendix 3 – Ethics List 47

Table of figures

Figure 1: Starbucks worldwide (Starbucks 2013) 7
Figure 2: Starbucks Logo (Starbucks 2013) 8
Figure 3: Customer Satisfaction Framework (Johnston 2012) 10
Figure 4: Decision Making Process (Noel 2009) 11
Figure 5: Research: Out of home hot drink purchase behaviour (Mintel 2012) 12
Figure 6: Research: Attitude towards coffee/tea/hot drinks out of home (Mintel 2012) 12
Figure 7: Service Quality Framework (Johnston 2012) 13
Figure 8: Conceptual Framework for the present research project (Schoja 2013) 14
Figure 9: Research onion related to this research (Saunders and Lewis 2012) 16
Figure 10: Research Process (Polonsky and Valler 2011) 17
Figure 11: Research Philisophy (Saunders and Lewis 2012) 17
Figure 12: Research Approaches (Burney 2008, Collins 2010) 18
Figure 13: Types of Studies (Saunders and Lewis 2012, Richey et al. 2007) 19
Figure 14: Research Strategies (Saunders and Lewis 2012) 19
Figure 15: Time Horizons (Saunders and Lewis 2012, Fitzmaurice et al. 2011) 20
Figure 16: Sampling methods (Oakshott 2012) 22
Figure 17: Pilot Test, Negative Critique, Question 5 25
Figure 18: Pilot Test, Negative Critique, Questions 6-8 25
Figure 19: Pilot Test, Positive Critique 26
Figure 20: Findings – Gender 27
Figure 21: Findings - Age 28
Figure 22: Findings – Place of Residence 28
Figure 23: Findings - Service quality factors in order of importance 29
Figure 24: Findings – Service Quality Factors in order of importance (Gender) ... 30
Figure 25: Findings - Decision Making Factors in order of importance 31
Figure 26: Findings – Decision Making Factors (Gender) 31
Figure 27: Findings – Consumer attitude towards Starbucks' tax avoidance (Age) 32
Figure 28: Findings – Consumer attitude towards taxes (Gender) 33
Figure 29: Findings – Consumer attitude towards Starbucks' tax avoidance 33
Figure 30: Findings – Consumer attitude towards Starbucks' tax avoidance (Integrity) 34
Figure 31: Findings - Consumer attitude towards Starbucks' tax avoidance (Place) 35
Figure 32: Findings - The first medium 36
Figure 33: Findings - Association 36
Figure 34: Conceptual Framework for the present research project (Schoja 2013) 37

Abstract

Due to the high supply on the market, companies have to investigate and understand customer needs to adapt their products or services and be competitive within the highly rival market. It is also initial to avoid any unethical behaviour as this may lead to retrogressive turnover.

This business research project focus on the investigation of factors which determine consumer behaviour within the catering industry. To concretise this extensive area, this work will concentrate on Starbucks' tax avoidance in the United Kingdom, which happened in December 2012.

As there are no relevant or current reports on Starbucks' tax avoidance and customer behaviour, the primary research on this issue will be done in this work. However the literature review provide a comprehensive review on relevant landmark studies of customer satisfaction and previous research on customer behaviour within the catering industry.

By means of self-provided conceptual framework and an appropriate methodology a quantitative online questionnaire were created and implemented. Findings from the primary research shows the importance of product quality for customers as well as less attention towards unethical behaviour of companies. Half of respondents who are aware of Starbuck's tax avoidance continue purchasing their products.

The research objectives, which were set at the beginning of the research are fully responded. This reflect the validity and reliability of this project.

According to the customer satisfaction, as the findings show the importance of quality, companies should maintain and reinforce the level of product quality to satisfy customers. Moreover a recommendation for Starbucks is to become aware of the issues of tax avoidance, apologize and get back their previous customers who boycott the company currently.

1. Introduction

1.1 The Purpose of this Research

The purpose of this research is to study consumer behaviour within the catering industry and to investigate the factors, which determine customer consumption preferences, as well as the main buying criteria for customers towards a hot drinks company. Due to Starbucks' tax avoidance in 2012 this research will examine whether the consumer perceive this matter as an important factor which influence their own decision making or not.

However, this research is focusing on a particular aspect 'tax avoidance within the catering industry' which has not been researched so well. There are not many studies on this certain issue. Therefore this research will study a specific issue within the overall complex of factors.

1.2 Structure of this Research

In the first chapter the literature will be reviewed, considering customer perception, expectation and satisfaction as well as the decision making process and the previous research, which has been done in this field.

In the following chapter the research methodology and the data collection process will be investigated and discussed. The primary data collection will be analysed in chapter 4, followed by a conclusion and recommendations.

To provide a better understanding to the reader, each chapter will be introduced and summarized at the end.

1.2 Research Questions

As O'Leary (2004) mentioned, a research questions is essential as "it gives focus, sets boundaries and provides directions". The questions for this research has been emerged from current developments in the industry and the extensive literature review, which has been done for the purpose of the research. The two main questions which have been conducted are:

1. What factors determine customer consumption preferences in the catering industry?

2. What are the main buying criteria for customers towards a hot drinks company?

1.3 Research Objectives

Well formulated objectives can be seen as a road map, which guide through a research project. They should be as specific and unambiguous as possible (MacDaniel 1998). Polonsky and Valler (2011) complements that objectives should be clear, achievable and will directly assist in answering the research question. To help in answering the research question within this project, following research objectives were formulated:

1. Investigate the determinants which affect the consumer behaviour and satisfaction and develop a conceptual framework for the research project based on previous studies. This objective will be met through collecting and analysing secondary data from academic text, industry reports and company website.

2. Examine the factors which determines the consumer decision making process, their perception and expectation. This objective will be met through collecting and analysing primary data, employing questionnaires as well as secondary data.

3. Explore how customers define service quality. This objective will be met through collecting and analysing primary data, employing questionnaires.

4. Observe consumer attitude towards an existing problem: tax avoidance of Starbucks. This objective will be met through collecting and analysing primary data, employing questionnaires.

1.4 Company Background

Starbucks is operating in the United States since 1971 and became a global organisation with nearly 18,000 retail stores in 2013, in 60 countries worldwide. The total net revenue in 2012 amounted to USD 13,3 billion. The mission of the company is "to inspire and nurture the human spirit – one person, one cup and one neighbourhood at a time" (Starbucks 2013).

Figure 1: Starbucks worldwide (Starbucks 2013)

The product range offered by Starbucks is wide and customized. Besides coffee and tea, the company sells handcrafted beverages like Frappuccino or smoothies, merchandise articles, as well as fresh food, including sandwiches, salads, yoghurt and ice cream (ibid.).

According to Jobber (2010), the Starbucks customer profile shows a young, single and high earner consumer. However, not only professionals and manager are their customers, but also students are an essential customer group. "The language is important for these consumers, where terms such as latte, cappuccino and espresso allow them to demonstrate connoisseurship" (ibid.).

Starbucks describes themselves as a responsible company, "always believed in the importance of building a great, enduring company that strikes a balance between profitability and a social conscience" (Starbucks 2013).

According to the Starbucks customer care policy, the company "strives to make every customer's experience pleasant and fulfilling, and they treat their customers as they treat one another, with respect and dignity. Furthermore a legendary customer service is a top priority at Starbucks". Even a Starbucks Ethics and Compliance Hotline is provided for the customer around the clock, all week long with no charges, and it is answered live. Here the customer can report any issues were ethics or legal issues are involved (Starbucks Coffee Company 2011)

Considering compliance with laws and regulations, Starbucks state to be committed to full compliance with the laws in every country where they operate and is committed to the highest ethical standards in all business transactions (ibid.) Therefore in 2013 and the previous 6 years the Ethisphere Institute (2013) has named Starbucks to the list of "world's most ethical companies'.

This show the importance of the company and deduce from that, that if the company is so important and it has so many customers worldwide, tax avoidance or any ethical issues related to the company will be multiplied.

In December 2012 many people in the UK were stunned at how little corporation tax Starbucks is paying (Murphy 2013). When Starbucks was asked why they pay so little in corporate income tax the answer was: "We do nothing illegal" (Babones 2012). This show that Starbucks do not perceive to have done something wrong.

Figure 2: Starbucks Logo (Starbucks 2013)

2. Literature Review
2.1 Overview
The critically selected literature review will study previous research on the topic, identify landmark studies and potential gaps in the academic literature. This research will explore past work in order to be able to develop a conceptual framework, which will assist in answering the research questions.

According to Ridley (2012) a literature review have to be done at the beginning of the research. It is even "one of the most important parts of any piece of academic writing, like a foundations upon which the rest of the work is build" (Oliver 2012). In fact a contribution to knowledge can be made through reviewing the literature (Easterby-Smith et al. 2011).

In this chapter the terminology and definitions from various authors will be critical investigated. Different approaches of customer's behaviour, customer perception and expectation as well as customer satisfaction will be critically discussed.

To get a better understanding of this research previous studies, which has been done up to this point, will be reviewed.

Moreover, the theoretical framework, which is relevant for this research, will be presented and complemented with essential factors to create a conceptual framework.

2.2 Relevant Literature
2.2.1 Customer Satisfaction and Dissatisfaction
A significant amount of work has been done so far on consumer behaviour, which is defined by Noel (2009) as "a process involved when consumer purchase, consumer and dispose goods so as to satisfy their needs".

Johnston (2012) describes a happy customer who would purchase more, towards an unhappy customer, so the company can sell more. These kind of customers are also the better listener and are already aware of the products the company offers, because of the trust (*ibid.*). On the other hand, if people are unhappy, first of all they will purchase less, but what is more important is the fact that they also will spread they unhappiness with others by word of mouth (Heppel 2010).

Similar to the previous definitions, Noel (2009) indicated a great performance of a product leads to encouragement of others to purchase through positive review as well as dissatisfaction which can lead to encourage to non-purchase through negative review. Even a boycott can be evoked by unsatisfied customers (*ibid.*)

To be able to make customers happy first we need to understand what exactly is customer satisfaction and how can it be measured. There are plenty of definitions of customer's satisfaction in the literature. Johnston (2012) defines customer satisfaction as an overall assessment of their perception compared to the expectation which they used to have before the purchase or the service delivery.

A framework which can be used to explain customer satisfaction, was developed by Johnston's (2012):

Figure 3: Customer Satisfaction Framework (Johnston 2012)

If the perception meets the expectation, the customer will be satisfied (Johnston 2012). In contrast to Johnston, Littman (2009) identified another way how some companies measure customer's satisfaction, where organisations measure the satisfaction by looking on how well they avoid customer's dissatisfaction, which is a mistake as not everyone who is not happy complains.

Additional to those authors, Ilhan (2010) stated in his quote that "companies need to give their customers what they want and not what companies think the customers might want, to get the customer coming back again and again".

This views provide different perspectives of the term 'customer satisfaction' and explores a number of aspects which influence customer's expectation and perception. This knowledge can be used to influence the consumer behaviour.

2.2.2 Customer's Expectation

In business we study customer's expectation to be able to influence them into the direction, we want our businesses to be developed, to be competitive, to increase profit as well as to stand out on the market we need to know what our customer's perceptions and expectations are.

On the market it is additional essential to retain customers, to be competitive. One of the reasons Stevens (2010) mentioned in his work is that you can earn the money back which an organisation have to spend to be the first and the longer you keep them, the more amount of investment will be paid off.

2.2.3 Customer's Perception

There are different personal factors how perception accrues. It could be personal experience with the brand or the product or the past, as well as culture, language, values, interests and assumptions. All these factor can affect customer's perception according to Johnston (2012). On the other hand expectations can be influenced by price, alternatives, marketing, word-of-mouth, previous experience, customers' mood and attitude and their confidence (ibid.)

Additional previous research has shown that satisfaction is heavily influenced by how the experiences felt when they were at their peak, best or worst, and how they felt when they ended. "If we create a good end to a service or a product, it is possible to manipulate the customer to a feeling of satisfaction" (Johnston 2012).

Kotler (2009) however, argued that "consumer themselves do not even know what exactly influences their purchases, because 95% of their thoughts which are responsible for purchases arise in the unconscious mind".

2.2.4 Consumer Behaviour Influences

According to Noel (2009) there are two different consumer behaviour influences: internal and external. The external influence includes the 4 P's and consumer culture, such religion, ethnicity, reference groups and social class. Where the internal includes the psychological (motivation, perception, attitude and knowledge) and decision making factors (problem solving, information search, judgement and decision making). After the purchase there is also post-decision process, which includes purchase and post-purchase behaviour.

In comparison to Noel (2009), Kotler (2009) is talking about 7 P's and other factors such culture, social, personal and psychological aspects. This factors cannot be controlled by marketers. He names the internal processes "buyer's black box", whose content needs to investigated.

2.2.5 Consumer Decision Making

Considering the consumer decision making process, a framework developed by various authors, describes how the usual decision making operates:

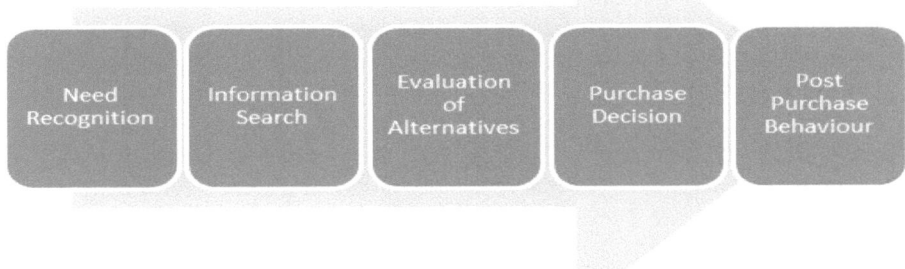

Figure 4: Decision Making Process (Noel 2009)

This framework mainly applies on expensive products, where for inexpensive products after problem recognition the customer make a decision without evaluating or collecting more information (Noel 2009, Kotler 2009). Jobber (2010) complements the evaluation and purchase stages using high and low involvement.

Consumer research in any case do not only help marketers to identify problems, in addition to it, it also helps to emerge opportunities (Noel 2009). Taking this into account this research will point out options, which catering industry, especially Starbucks, can use to increase customer satisfaction and influence customer's decision making.

2.2.6 Previous Research on Consumer Behaviour within the Catering Industry

As we can see from the previous research below, Figure 5, in December 2011, Starbucks was the second largest brand within "out of home hot drink purchase" close behind Costa Coffee, which might be caused by different perceptions and expectations.

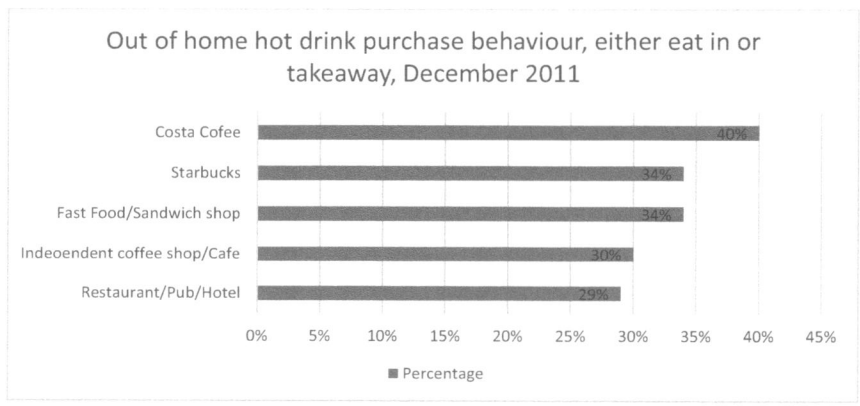

Figure 5: Research: Out of home hot drink purchase behaviour (Mintel 2012)

Considering the next research findings, Figure 6 shows us that 66% of the respondents stated that the 'quality' is the most important factor when buying coffee out of home. However as we have discussed before it is essential to define quality first.

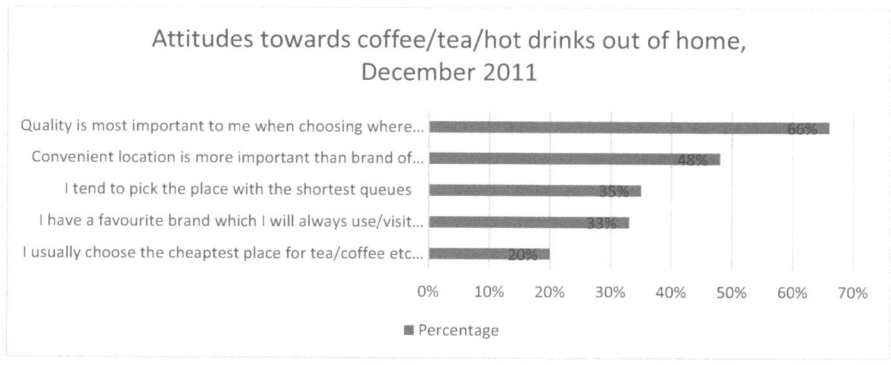

Figure 6: Research: Attitude towards coffee/tea/hot drinks out of home (Mintel 2012)

2.2.7 Service Quality

According to Johnston (2012), customer satisfaction can be managed while influencing customer perceptions and expectations. By doing so it is needed to understand how exactly the customer perceive quality followed by influencing customer's expectation. The service quality framework which is used by Johnston contains following factors:

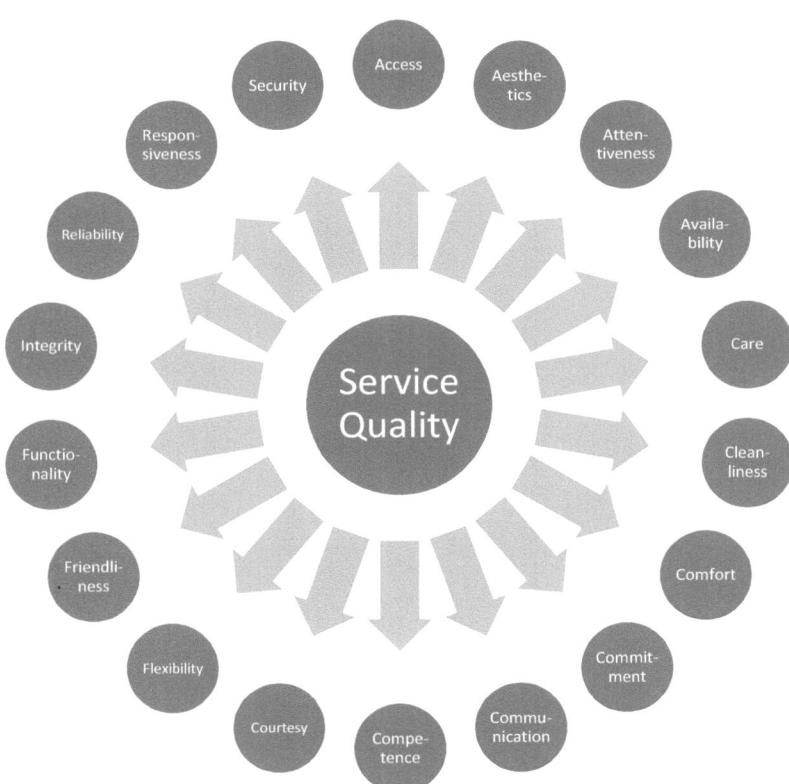

Figure 7: Service Quality Framework (Johnston 2012)

This theoretical framework is used to create the conceptual framework for this research.

2.2.8 Conceptual Framework

According to Kumar (2010) "a conceptual framework stems from the theoretical framework and focuses on the section which become the basis of the study". This research is based on theoretical framework, Figure 7, developed by Johnston (2012), which explores the quality factors. The conceptual framework, Figure 8, will investigate the most significant factors from the theoretical framework as well as supplementary factors which are essential for customers within the catering industry.

Based on the work of Johnston (2012), this research has identify following factors which should be studied. This will help in answering the research questions: Availability of service; Comfort of facilities; Competence of staff; Courtesy; Flexibility – Willingness to meet customer needs; Integrity - Honesty and trustworthiness with which customer are treated by the organisation; Responsiveness – Speed of service delivery.

To specify the questionnaire according to the case, two additional factors will be enclosed: Knowing the customer – Ability to provide the best service; Appearance of personnel. The two additional factors are important as these concepts apply to the catering industry as well as to Starbucks, since the company is highly specialized on customer needs as well as appearance.

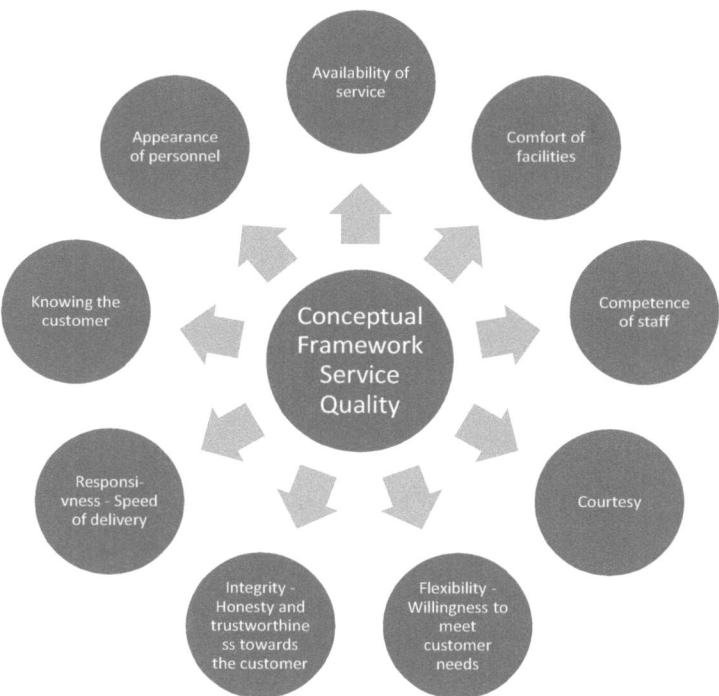

Figure 8: Conceptual Framework for the present research project (Schoja 2013)

This conceptual framework allows us to develop the questionnaire, focusing on the specific categories of interest.

2.3 Conclusion of the Literature Review

This literature review highlights the landmarks which are relevant for this study. Customer satisfaction and dissatisfaction were discussed looking at the customer satisfaction framework developed by Johnston (2012) and complemented by Noel (2009), Heppel (2010) and Stevens (2010).

Furthermore, according to Noel (2009) and Kotler (2009), two customer behaviour influences were investigated, external and internal. Both authors stated similar definitions, supplementing each other's work by additional factors.

Decision making process framework was acquired by various authors. This show a similar thinking. However, Jobber (2010) addresses the evaluation and purchase stages in depth, distinguished between low and high involvement.

From the previous research (Mintel 2012) it can be inferred that Costa Coffee and Starbucks are top of mind brands and the most important factor for customers within the coffee industry is the 'quality'.

There might be no industry report written on the specific topic 'Starbucks tax avoidance' as this matter is too recent.

Using the most relevant factors from the theoretical service quality framework (Johnston 2012) and adding two more factors, a conceptual framework has been created. This will be applied for the questionnaire to answer the research question.

The landmark studies are essential for this research and can be used effectively for the primary research as well as a guide for the research objectives.

3. Research Methodology

3.1 Overview

In the previous chapter the relevant and available literature has been reflected. Tthis chapter will depict the relevant methodology for the collection of primary and secondary data, using the research onion, defined by Saunders and Lewis (2012). Moreover different approaches will be discussed as well as various collecting data opportunities.

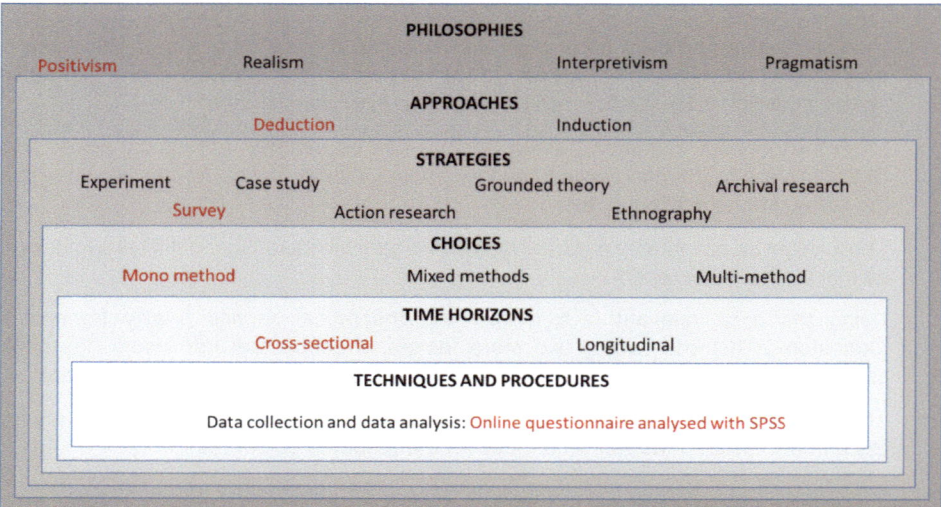

Figure 9: Research onion related to this research (Saunders and Lewis 2012)

As Kothari (2008) suggested, not only knowing the research techniques is important but also be acquainted with the methodology. This can be describes as a way to methodically solve the research problem and to answer the research questions:

1. What factors determine customer consumption preferences in the catering industry?

2. What are the main buying criteria for customers towards a hot drinks company?

The sections below will justify the choice of a methodology.

3.2 Research Process

As Polonsky and Valler (2011) stated, it is essential to understand and follow the research process, which includes six steps:

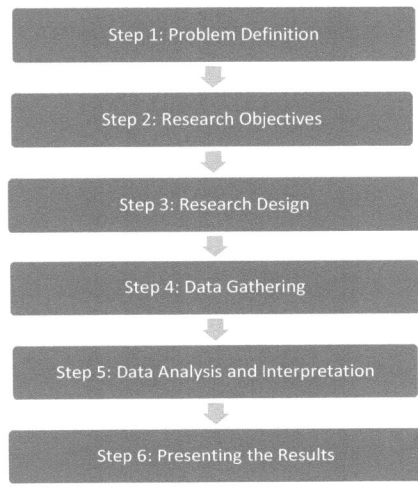

Figure 10: Research Process (Polonsky and Valler 2011)

3.2 Research Design
3.2.1 Research Philosophy

As Saunders and Lewis (2012) argue, there are 4 available research philosophies which can be used: positivism, realism, interpretivism and pragmatism.

A research philosophy can be described as the way how researcher see the world around them. As distinguished from Saunders and Lewis, Collis and Hussey (2009, p. 55) argue that "a research paradigm is a philosophical framework that guide how scientific research should be conducted", and is whether 'positivism' or 'interpretivism'. Additional mixed method 'pragmatism' should be the key factor in determining methodology according to some researchers.

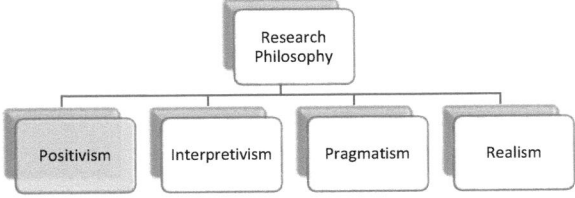

Figure 11: Research Philisophy (Saunders and Lewis 2012)

Within the positivism research philosophy observable and measurable variables are investigated, were replications are allowed. This philosophy can be observed mostly within the physical and natural science (Saunders and Lewis 2012).

Those authors support the view of Collis and Hussey (2009, p.56) who constitute that 'positivism' rests on the assumption that social reality is singular and objective. This research philosophy support a deductive approach with a view to providing explanatory theories to understand social phenomena. Quantitative methods are used by positivists.

On the other hand interpretivism rests on the assumption that social reality is on our minds only, and is subjective. This research philosophy is based on the inductive process (ibid.) An interpretive research is, according to Strauss and Corbin (1990), one type of research where findings are not deduced from the statistical analysis of quantitative data.

For pragmatism the most important aspects are the research questions and the research objectives (Saunders and Lewis 2012). Therefore, Collis and Hussey (2009, p.66) argue to mix 'positivism' and 'interpretivism' together to 'pragmatism' to be able to gain useful and significant findings and not only to stock on a single paradigms.

As positivism assume that social reality is singular and objective this research will use positivism as a philosophy.

3.2.2 Research Approaches

At the next onion stage two research approaches are given: deduction and induction. As Burney (2008) mentioned, deduction begins with the general and end with the specific, whereas induction is vice versa.

Collins (2010) specifies deductive approach, where the research needs to be independent of what is being observed and the researcher have to be objective. Any personal feelings or views of the researcher should not enter into the research.

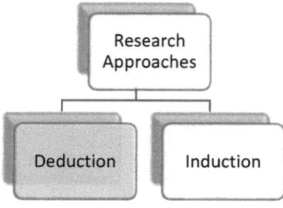

Figure 12: Research Approaches (Burney 2008, Collins 2010)

As for this research objectivity is needed, deduction is the more appropriate approach.

3.2.3 Types of Studies

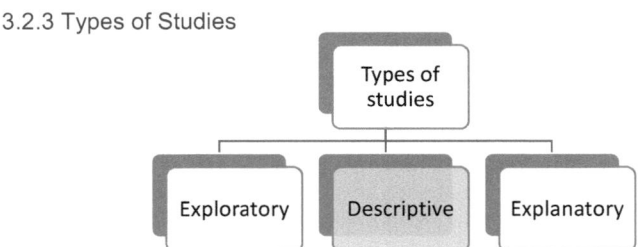

Figure 13: Types of Studies (Saunders and Lewis 2012, Richey et al. 2007)

Three different types of studies have to be discussed at this stage. The most appropriate study will be used in this research.

The first study, exploratory, is used when a researcher wish to obtain information about an issue that is not clearly understood so far (Saunders and Lewis 2012). For this reason, as Richey et al. (2007) mentioned in their investigation, that there are not many guidelines to follow and the research is less structured than in descriptive research.

Investigating the next two studies, descriptive is the previous step of explanatory study. Descriptive study includes measurable data and is describing facts only, without an explanation why something is like that, where the explanatory study explains the relationship between variables and is used in case studies or statistical surveys. (Saunders and Lewis 2012)

This research will use a descriptive study to describe facts only.

3.2.4 Research Strategies

To be able to decide which strategy is the most appropriate it is needed to examine all of them first. Various strategies can be used in the research, or even combined strategies.

Figure 14: Research Strategies (Saunders and Lewis 2012)

Considering the experiment it shows whether a link between variables exist or not. This means that if there is a change in one variable, will this cause a change in the other variable or not (Saunders and Lewis 2012). Dul and Hak (2008) complements that within an experiment one or more variables are manipulated. Regarding this explanation, this strategy is not suitable.

Survey as a strategy where data from questionnaires, structured observation and structured interviews is collected and it is the most applicable in business research (ibid.). Denscombe (2007) argues that those researcher who use survey as a strategy are able to use many different methods, for example questionnaires, interviews and observation. It can be seen as a „combination of a commitment to a breadth of study, a focus on the snapshot at a given point in time and a dependence on empirical data". As a questionnaire has standardized questions this strategy is appropriate for this research and will be used to collect primary data and answer the research objectives.

A case study is using multiple source of evidence, it goes more into detail to get deep understanding of the research topic (Johnston 2012), and it uses a real life context (Dul and Hak 2008).

An action research is not suitable due to the length of time, which is needed. Similar to the action research a grounded theory is not appropriate as well. This theory is developed from data which were obtained from observations or interviews (Saunders and Lewis 2012).

The key concept of ethnography is to learn from people rather than to study them (Saunders and Lewis 2012). Fetterman (2010) complements that ethnography gives voice to people in their own local context. But as this strategy is time consuming, it is not suitable to our 10 weeks research.

An archival research is using administrative records and documents which already exist (Saunders and Lewis 2012). Due to the fact that such data and information do not exist, this strategy will not be used in this research.

3.2.5 Time Horizons

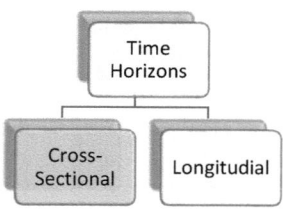

Figure 15: Time Horizons (Saunders and Lewis 2012, Fitzmaurice et al. 2011)

Considering the time horizons there are cross-sectional research and longitudinal studies. Saunders and Lewis (2012) describes cross-sectional research as a study over a particular period of time, a snapshot, where longitudinal study investigates a topic over extended period of time. Measurements of the same individuals are taken repeatedly through time and allow changes over time (Fitzmaurice et al. 2011).

Due to the time limitation of ten weeks only, the cross-sectional time dimension will be used for this research.

3.2.6 Techniques and Procedures

According to Collis and Hussey (2009) primary data are „data generated from an original source, whereas secondary data have been collected from an existing source".

The difference between quantitative and qualitative is that qualitative data are data in a nominal form were quantitative are data in a numerical form. Furthermore qualitative will provide the depth of information of data, while the quantitative provides the breadth. Using the quantitative approach it is possible to survey a lot of people.

To collect primary data for this research ideally the combination of quantitative questionnaires and qualitative interviews would be suitable. However, because of the limitations of this research the decision was made to focus on questionnaires, and to conduct interviews only if there is another additional stage of this research.

3.3 Primary Data Collection Process

According to Flick (2011), advantage of quantitative research is that it is possible to investigate a higher number of cases within short time given and the results have a high degree of generalizability.

However, the benefits of qualitative research is the detailed and in-depth analysis, in which "participants have much more freedom to determine what is relevant for them and to present it in its contexts". In contrast, Kothari (2008) simplify the difference to quantitative research which is based on the measurement of quality, where qualitative research is concerned with qualitative phenomenon.

Going more in detail, Kumar (2010) stated, that questionnaire questions can be concepts or variables, where a variables are measurable and concepts are "mental images or perceptions and therefore their meanings vary markedly from individual to individual"

In this research the variables are gender, age, and place of residence. On the other hand, concepts are the questions about the perception of various quality factors and attitude against Starbuck's tax avoidance.

Using a pilot test a questionnaire can be verified for weaknesses and errors, which will be improved before the implementation (Kothari 2008). Furthermore, Saunders and Lewis (2012) highlighted, that a pilot test will avoid disappointments within the current data collection. The accomplished pilot test for this research will be discussed in detail in the next chapter.

As Flick (2011) mentioned in his work, a new trend on doing research has arisen: 'online research', which brings new opportunities as well as challenges. The most evident advantages for using online questionnaires are costs, time, as well as the absence of geographical and temporal boundaries (Wright 2005).

Skiadas (2009) supplemented the advantage list by identifying the major advantage that "results are collated by the programme used so that the researcher can immediately start to analyse the findings after the data collection phase. Additional advantage is the evidence to say „online questionnaires obtain a higher number of respondents than paper based questionnaires"(ibid).

For this research an online questionnaire has been created to collect primary quantitative data. By using www.q-set.cu.uk, a free online survey website, 9 concept and variables questions were prepared, one of them is an open question.

3.3.1 Sampling

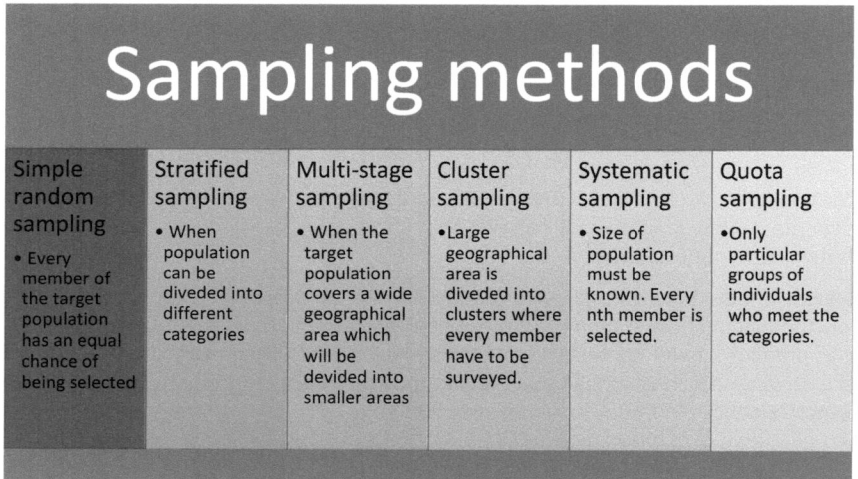

Figure 16: Sampling methods (Oakshott 2012)

The questionnaire was spread online by using social media as a prime source. To be able to focus on London and to ensure collecting random samples only, the link to the questionnaire were placed on London's specific Facebook groups, like 'London City' or 'Germans living in London', which has between 1,000 and 15,000 members, trying to get as many completed questionnaires returned as possible.

Random sampling is according to Oakshott (2012) a method where every single participant of the target population has an equal chance of being selected. This sampling strategy will be used in this research, to make sure not to manipulate the findings.

After the collection, there are different options to analyse the data. A common method is to use Excel, which also produce immediately changeable, professional charts. Another option is SPSS which is used analysing the findings in this research as this programme provide statistical packages (Oakshott 2012) and is possibly the most widely used computer software for the analysis of quantitative data within business research (Bryman and Bell 2011).

SPSS will be used in this research as it is a more appropriate method with statistical packages.

3.4 Validity
'Validity is the extent to which the research findings reflect the phenomena under study' (Collis and Hussey 2009 p. 64). Being more specific, Saunders and Lewis (2012), describes that "validity is concerned with whether the findings are really about what they appear to be about or not". Validity is about promising what exactly the researcher is going to do. Researching what have been said to be researched.

This research addresses the validity by providing a comprehensive literature review and release a list of factors of categories based on which the conceptual framework has been created. The literature review is following the research objectives which has been set.

Therefore the objectives have also been linked with the conceptual framework, with specific research methodology which have been chosen, with the findings and linking those with the recommendations. This research design on purpose was done to ensure to meet the research objectives.

Validity is about using the online means to distribute the questionnaire but also having an extensive database which can be provided upon request. However, a sample can be found in the appendix.

3.5 Reliability
According to Collis and Hussey (2009, p. 64) reliability refers to the absence of differences in the result if the research were repeated. Garmines and Zeller (1979), confirm this statement by considering that "reliability concerns the extent to which an experiment yields the same result on repeated trials". Reliability is very important in positivism studies.

Saunders and Lewis (2012) describes reliability as an extent where the data collection methods and the analysis provide consistent findings. This research has to be transparent as well as that everyone should be able to replicate it. The findings of this research are consistent. A sample of the findings can be found in the appendices, were a full list of findings can be provided upon request.

3.6 Generalizability
Generalizability is „the extent to which the research findings can be extended to other cases or other settings"(Collis and Hussey 2009, p. 65). However, Gummersson (1991) argues that using statistics to generalize from a sample to a bigger population is just one type of generalization which can be used.

3.7 Ethical Issues
In the investigation of Saunders and Lewis (2012), research ethics are the adequacy of the researcher towards the rights of the respondents or potential subject of a research project. As no research should cause harm it is essential to consider and respect many ethical aspects while implementing a research.

In this research, before partaking in advance, the participants have been made aware of the confidentiality of information and anonymity as in the cover letter it says that all the information the respondent provide will be treated highly confidentially as the results will be used in summary form only. Moreover the respondents are aware not to be asked to include any personal details in the questionnaire, for example name or address. Additional, no identifying information will be shared in the analysis. Therefore there are no risks associated with participating in this study.

The initial information about the purpose of this research was explained to the respondents by describing the topic and the significance of the participation. However, it is explained that this questionnaire is absolutely voluntary and if the respondent do not want to continue filling the questionnaire. They are free to refuse it at any given time without justification.

To consider the precious time of the respondents, the average required time, 5 minutes only, was stated in the cover letter. This show the awareness of ethical issue, honestly and give the respondents the choice to take part or not.

Moreover, by providing contact data, every potential participant is able to get in contact to get further information about the research or to ask any question.

All the issues have been addressed in the cover letter of the questionnaire. A sample can be found in the appendices.

3.6 Limitations

An important limitation of this research is the time limitation. Within 10 weeks it is crucial to choose an appropriate topic and suitable strategy and methods. Therefore the decision was made to implement a quantitative method, online questionnaire, only, instead of conducting quantitative and qualitative methods which would provide in-depth and in-breadth information. This method would also be problematic due to the analysis, as the time would be not sufficient.

There was no previous research done on Starbucks' tax avoidance, which is a limitation. It is not possible to compare and contrast critically the findings from this research with previous research as Starbucks' tax avoidance is a recent issue.

As the research is done from another country, it is implemented online rather than personally. Issues can occur as not every participant answer all questions and it is not possible for respondents to ask questions if they have some while filling out the questionnaire. However, an advantage from the online questionnaire is the higher participants' number. While online respondents can fill out the questionnaire at the same time, with a face-to-face interview respondents could only answer consecutively. This would take more time to get acceptable number of respondents.

Due to the online questionnaire, an additional limitation occurs, which is the age of respondents. The questionnaire was spread via Facebook, which is used by young people the most. Nevertheless, as this research address the company Starbucks, this age group is appropriate since Starbucks customers are described as young, single, high earner consumer, not only professionals and managers, but also students are an essential customer group (Jobber 2010).

4. Findings, Interpretation and Discussion
4.1 Pilot Test Findings
By conducting a pilot test with seven pilot respondents, it was vital to find out whether the questionnaire contains mistakes or the respondents easily understand the meaning of the questions.

The feedback and the modification on the pilot questionnaire can be found in the next paragraphs

4.1.1 Negative Critique, Question 5

Pilot 1:
"It is brilliant, but I am wondering about two rows which are about 'Value for money'. I think that it is mix of price and product quality so if you could write 'value for money' instead, it is going to be better."

Modification: Delete the factor 'Value for money' and focus on 'price' and 'quality' only, as these factors have to be examine individually.

Figure 17: Pilot Test, Negative Critique, Question 5

4.1.2 Negative Critique, Questions 6-8

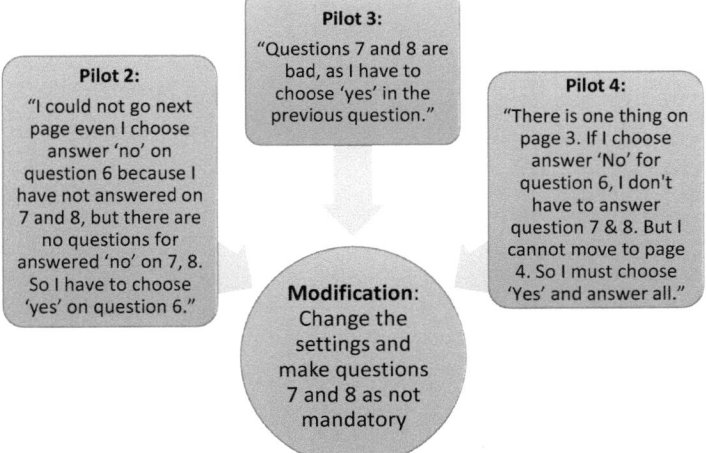

Pilot 2:
"I could not go next page even I choose answer 'no' on question 6 because I have not answered on 7 and 8, but there are no questions for answered 'no' on 7, 8. So I have to choose 'yes' on question 6."

Pilot 3:
"Questions 7 and 8 are bad, as I have to choose 'yes' in the previous question."

Pilot 4:
"There is one thing on page 3. If I choose answer 'No' for question 6, I don't have to answer question 7 & 8. But I cannot move to page 4. So I must choose 'Yes' and answer all."

Modification: Change the settings and make questions 7 and 8 as not mandatory

Figure 18: Pilot Test, Negative Critique, Questions 6-8

4.1.3 Positive Critique

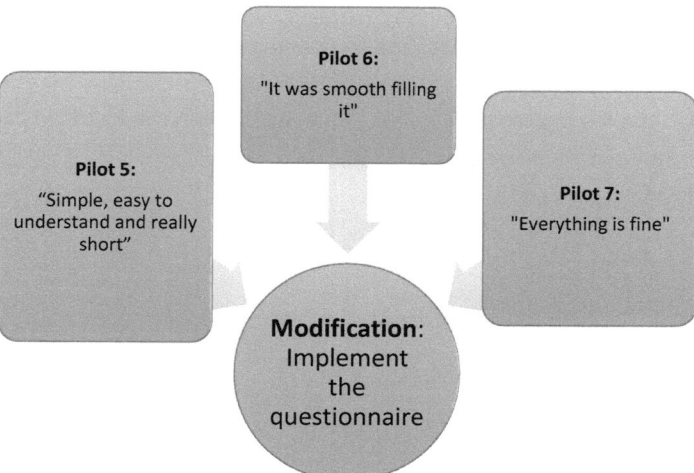

Figure 19: Pilot Test, Positive Critique

4.2 Findings, Interpretation and Discussion

The questionnaire has been created at the website www.q-set.co.uk, where 161 questionnaires have been fully completed, 50 questionnaires have been started, but not fully completed and 149 times a questionnaire have been called up without being answering at all. This show an overall participation of 45%.

For the sake of completeness, only those questionnaires which have been fully completed will be used for the SPSS analysis. 161 respondents partaken the survey.

The findings, interpretation and discussion will be presented interconnected in the next paragraphs.

4.2.1 General - Questions 1-3

46% of the respondents are male and the majority with 54% are female as we can see from Figure 20. This show a gender-neutral allocation.

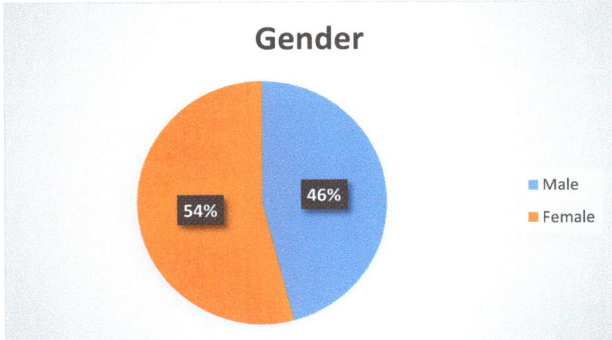

Figure 20: Findings – Gender

Figures 21 and 22 describe the age allocation as well as place of residence. The major age group is between 16 and 24 years old with 48%, followed by 25 to 34 years old with 36%. This result is attributable on the type of data collection, as younger people seems to use social media more often and more intensive than the older generation.

This is a limitation of this research since more young people, 50% of the respondents, have filled in the questionnaire. The social network Facebook was used where mostly young people are members, which limited the access to other age groups to this research.

In the previous research from Mintel (2012), all respondents were +16, which is different to this research due to the random sampling method, as it is unavoidable to get response from a specific age group only.

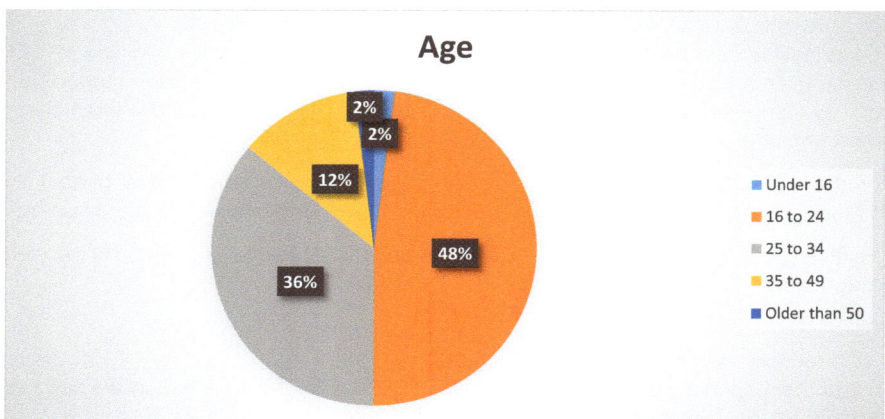

Figure 21: Findings - Age

Focusing on London only, in this research most respondents are from the capital of United Kingdom, which amounts to 85%. To make this possible, the link to the questionnaire were distributed to London specific Facebook-groups only. This is crucial for this research, as it might be assumed that people outside the United Kingdom are not aware of Starbucks' tax avoidance and cannot participate this research.

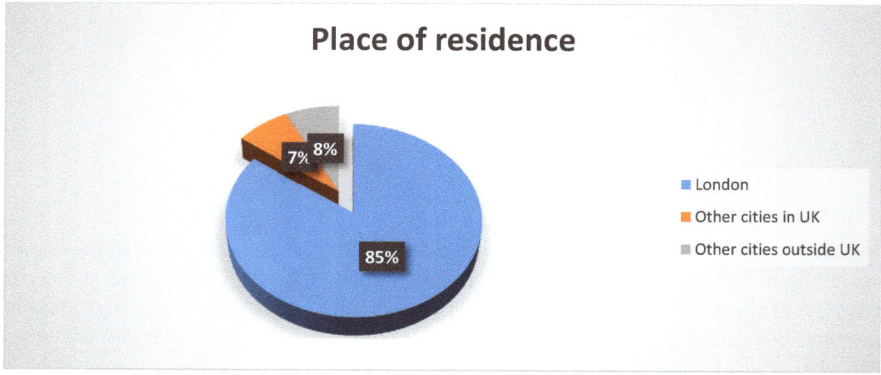

Figure 22: Findings – Place of Residence

Nevertheless, when using a simple random sampling even if the questionnaire were distributed to London specific Facebook-groups only, it is not possible to prevent respondents from other cities or even countries as the access to the Facebook-groups is not limited.

4.2.2 Consumer Behaviour Service Quality - Question 4

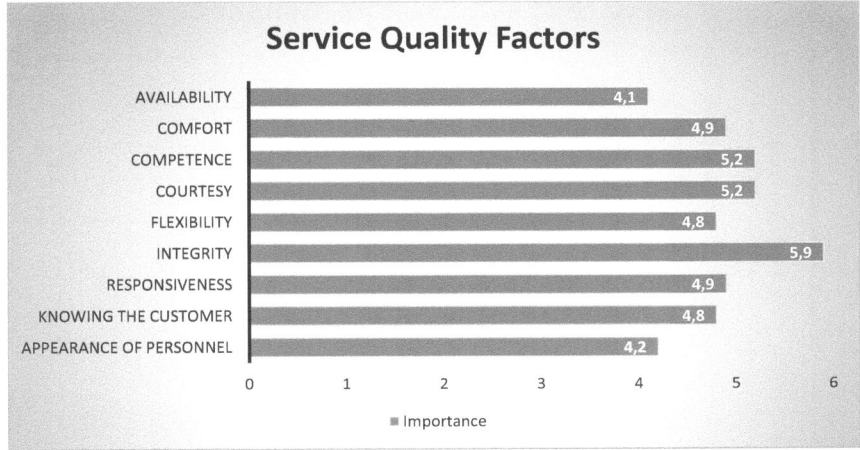

Figure 23: Findings - Service quality factors in order of importance (0 = not important; 6 = very important)

Figure 23 shows the conceptual framework 'service quality factors' and the importance for the respondents. By filling this question, respondents were asked to rank all the factors in order of importance, where 0 is not important and 6 is very important.

Integrity – honesty and trustworthiness with which customers are treated by the organisation – were stated as the most important factor, scored with 5.9 out of 6, followed by competence and courtesy of employees, with 5.2. Availability of services provided by the company were stated as least important.

This finding describes in a direct way what consumer perceive as the most essential factors and aspects. Availability of service is not important nowadays as many hot drinks chains provide similar services.

This findings has been confirmed by Johnston, who also claims that customer's plays huge importance on the integrity, competence and courtesy.

The findings in Figure 23 give an overview of how consumer rank the quality factors in general. However, the next Figure 24 is specified by gender. There is nearly no difference for females, as they stated almost all factors as 'important', except the factor 'appearance'. Male, on the other hand display wide variations, ranking the factors.

From this Figure it can be said that male perceive integrity as the most important factors, thus, the overall 'integrity' factor is stated as the most important.

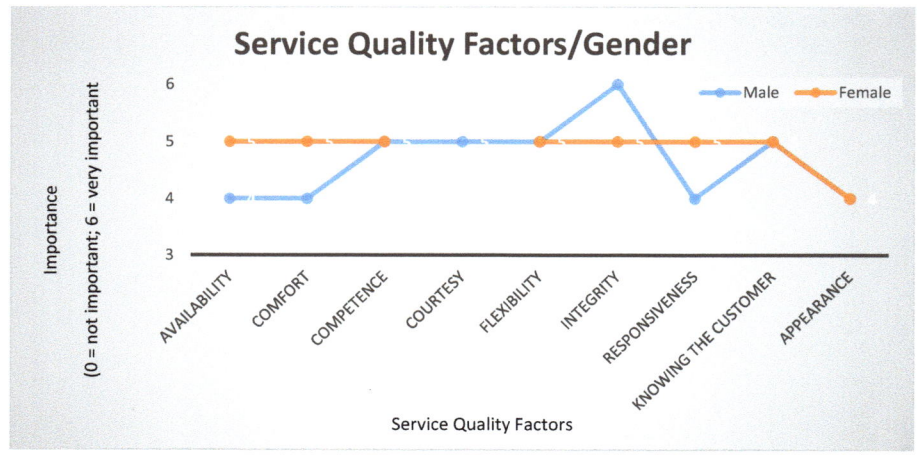

Figure 24: Findings – Service Quality Factors in order of importance (Gender)

The importance of the factors seems to have not been addressed by any of the previous research, as the integrity has not been the most important factor before. This might be referable to outdated data or outdated research, where consumer's preferences differ from present-day attitudes. Over time customer needs and wants changes with the environment. Companies should consider this important aspect and should be able to adapt timely.

Using those figured a company can manage customer satisfaction by influencing customer expectation and perception as stated by Johnston (2012).

4.2.3 Consumer Behaviour Decision Making - Question 5

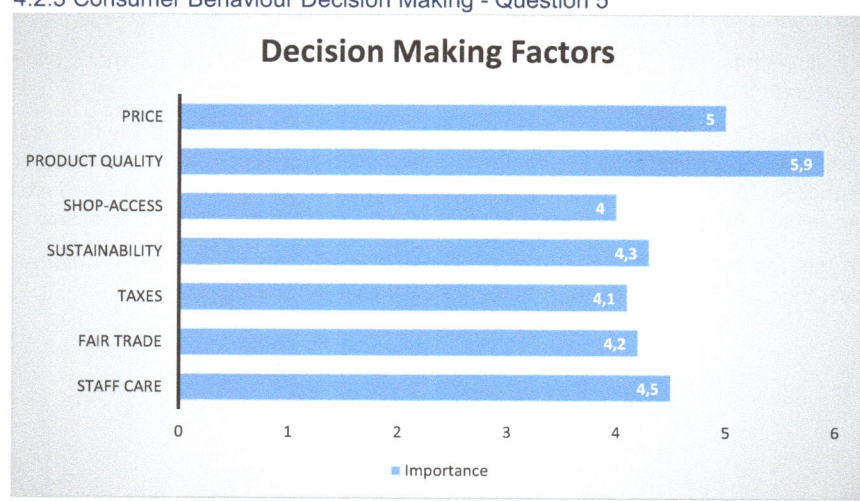

Figure 25: Findings - Decision Making Factors in order of importance (0 = not important; 6 = very important)

From Figure 25 we can see which factors are essential for consumer decision making. The respondents were asked to rank the importance of the seven factors below, where 0 means not important and 6 is very important.

Customers highly prefer good quality products and services, followed by low prices. This show that customers not only wish value for money, but rather are willing to pay higher prices to get the quality they wish.

At least important factor is 'shop-access' ranked with 4 out of 6, which means that respondents do not highly prefer shops which they can access and find easily. This response might be attributed to the fact that the respondents not clearly understood this aspect and allocated the lowest possible grade, even it was explained in the questionnaire.

Another concept why 'shop-access' is not important is the location. Most respondents are from London where there are many hot drink chains available. Consumer do not have the problem to find a shop as the density of shops is high in London.

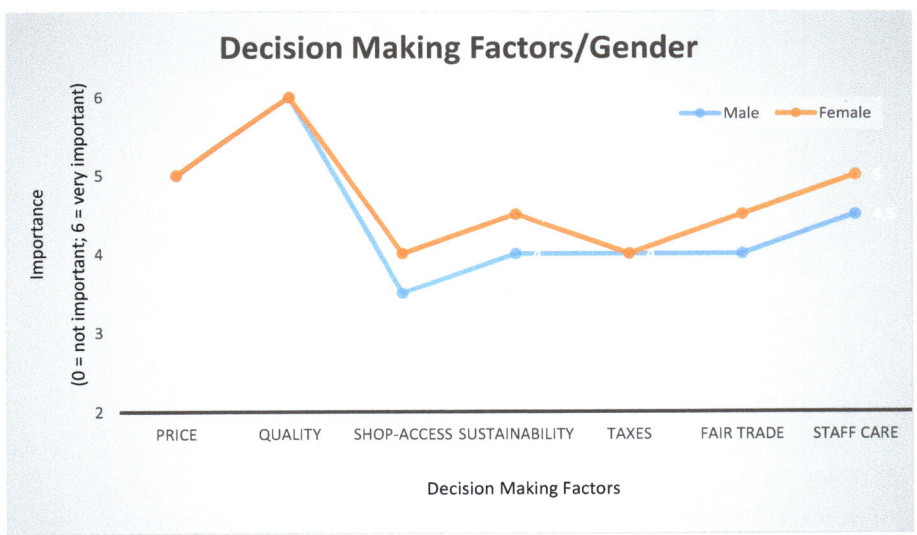

Figure 26: Findings – Decision Making Factors (Gender)

Figure 26 is considering decision making factors divided by gender. As distinguished from the service quality factors in Figure 24, here a clear relation between male and female can be seen. Quality is the most essential factor for both, were shop-access and taxes are less important.

As shown in the previous research in the literature review, quality were listed as the most important determinant as well. Due to the independence from each other it can be said, that customer perceive 'quality' as a key factor within the decision making.

4.2.4. Consumer Behaviour Taxes – Question 5

In Figure 27 a correlation between age groups and the importance for the consumer, whether a company is paying taxes or not, is presented. Due to the low respondents in the age group 'Under 16' and '50 or older', the findings are not significant. Considering the three remaining age groups it can be said, that there is no clear preferences, as the numbers are widely spread. However, a tendency to medium importance is stated by most respondents.

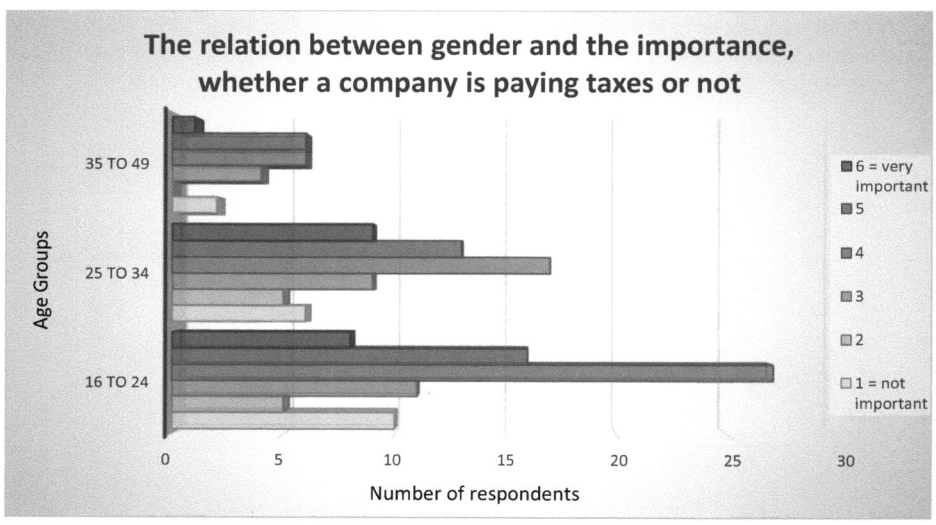

Figure 27: Findings – Consumer attitude towards Starbucks' tax avoidance (Age)

Considering this results it can be said, that the aspect whether a company behave ethical or not is not significantly for the majority.

However, in the following paragraph a tendency to avoid buying products from a company which behave unethical will show the opposite of this results. Certainly, it might rests on the specific company, Starbucks, only. This argument amend the previous contradiction.

Alike to the previous table, in Figure 28 is the relation between gender and the importance, whether the company is paying taxes or not.

As distinguished from the previous table, a clear trend can be seen. Females experience the taxation of company as more important than males. In total there is more females stated the importance with 4 and 5, which is located in the higher stage of importance.

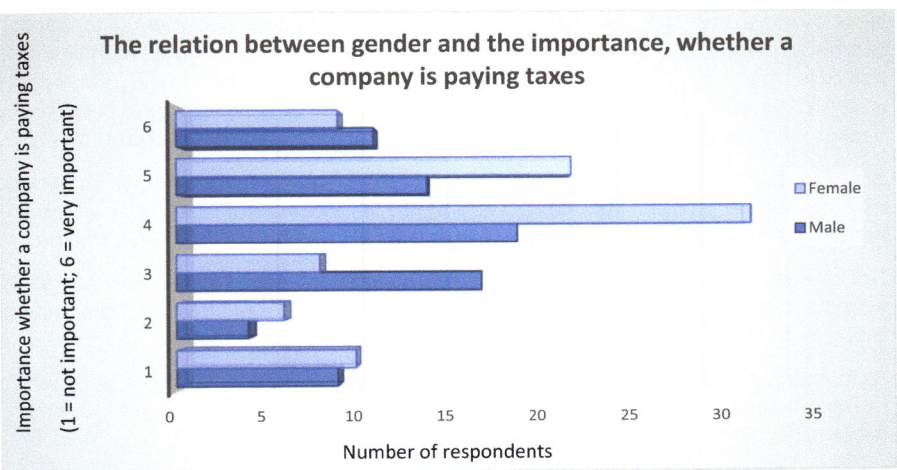

Figure 28: Findings – Consumer attitude towards taxes (Gender)

4.2.4 Starbucks - Questions 6-9

Figure 29 investigate whether people which have heard of Starbucks' tax avoidance, prevent buying Starbucks products or not. There is no precise attitude as almost 50% answered with 'yes', which means another 50% for 'no'.

Figure 29: Findings – Consumer attitude towards Starbucks' tax avoidance

This is something which was not found in the literature published In English. This is an issues which has to be persecute further.

Nevertheless, this is a high number of customers who are considering to boycott Starbucks. Generalizing this sample to all Starbucks' customers would signifies, that half of them are avoiding the company due to the tax avoidance in 2012. This reflects a high customer involvement and high risk for businesses. As mentioned in company background any ethical issues will be multiplied due to the big size of the company.

Specified findings from Figure 29 can be founded in Figure 30. It describes customers who are aware of Starbucks' tax avoidance regarding the importance of integrity – honesty and trustworthiness with which customers are treated by the organisation.

Not all respondents who stated to perceive integrity as very important (6 out of 6), would avoid to buy Starbucks' products. Only 20 out of 32 would boycott the company which is contradiction to their previous statement to the factor integrity.

Respondents who quote to perceive integrity as important (4 and 5 out of 6) would rather not avoid buying Starbucks' products. 44 out of 68 would continue purchasing those products.

According to this figures it can be assumed that customers interpret 'integrity' different. Honestly and trustworthiness can be defined distinct from every individual

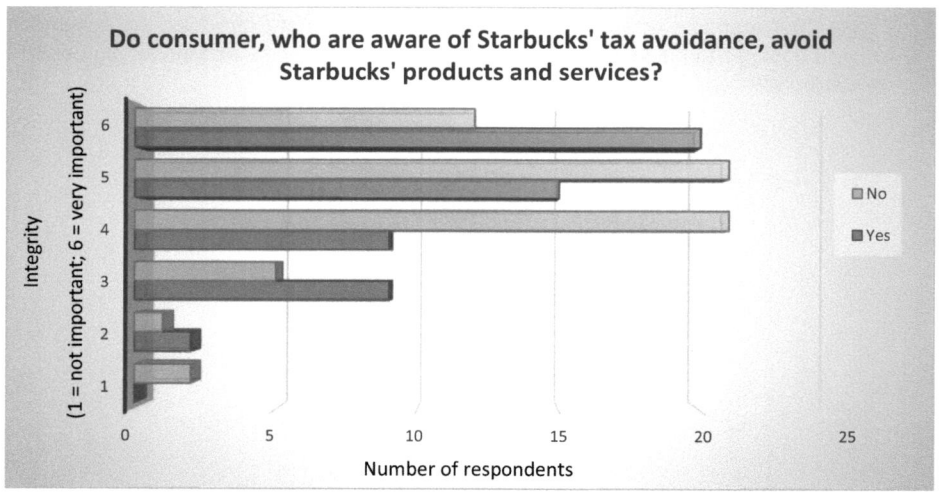

Figure 30: Findings – Consumer attitude towards Starbucks' tax avoidance (Integrity)

As mentioned before, this questionnaire was primary created for residents from London. However, Figure 31 illustrates other two categories of residents, from other cities in the United Kingdom and outside the United Kingdom.

People living in London tend to become less anxious about the tax avoidance. On the other hand, people from other cities in the United Kingdom would rather not consume or purchase Starbucks products. Those people seems to pay less attention on issues regarding a company with unethical behaviour.

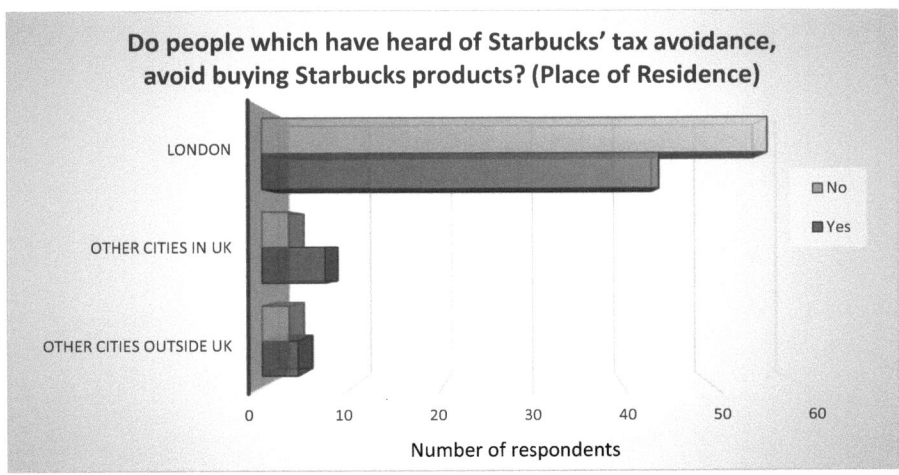

Figure 31: Findings: Consumer attitude towards Starbucks' tax avoidance (Place of Residence)

Figure 32 shows the medium where the respondents heard of Starbucks' tax avoidance for the first time. Newspaper, with 45% is the most listed medium, followed by online news and television.

Focusing mostly on London this results have been reinforce due to the fact that people in London have access to the newspaper 'Metro' and 'Evening Standard' free of charge two times a day. Such a massive and shocking news about Starbuck's tax avoidance were spread rapidly. Other newspapers also reported about this topic.

This results display the medium with the fastest distribution in London, even though online news or channels would be assumed as fastest medium.

Using this results, companies can response to their customers in case of an issues more effective. Although an online statement would be more flexible and more favourable, an organisation should consider using newspapers where they can reach wide customer base faster. 'Evening Standard or 'Metro' are appropriate, as here companies can easily react. 'Tesco' apologized in this way, after the horse meat scandal was released (Metro 2013).

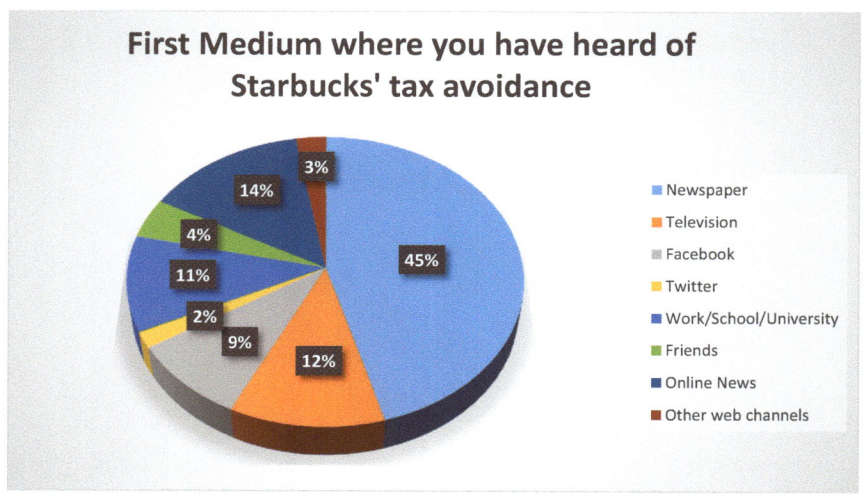

Figure 32: Findings – The first medium where consumer have heard of Starbucks' tax avoidance

4.2.5 Association – Question 9

Participants were asked to name five, or as many as they can, coffee/tea chains they associate with hot drinks. A full list of information can be provided upon request.

In terms of the association, the respondents named mostly Starbucks (27%), followed by Costa Coffee (14%) and Café Nero (13%). Customers also quoted Pret a Manger, McCafe and Eat.

Due to the repeated mentions of Starbucks in previous questions of the questionnaire, this figure might be manipulated. However, considering the previous research which has been reported on Mintel (2012), Starbucks was the second largest brand within 'out of home hot drink purchase' close behind Costa Coffee.

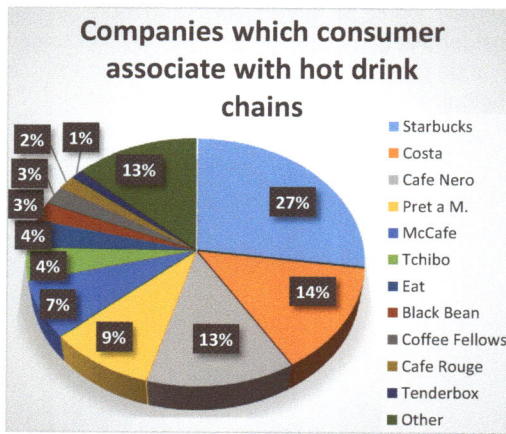

This reflect the reliability of this project as both, previous and current research release nearly the same results.

Starbucks and Costa Coffee gained top-of-mind awareness within the hot drink industry. A top-of-mind is the brand which is considered first by customers (Kotler 2009).

Figure 33: Findings - Association

5. Conclusion

The research objectives which were set at the beginning of this research have been met and are highlighted in the literature review as well as in the primary research findings and discussion.

For the first objective 'Investigate the determinants which affect the consumer behaviour and satisfaction and develop a conceptual framework for the research project based on previous studies.' a conceptual framework have been created based on Johnston' (2012) theoretical service quality framework:

Figure 34: Conceptual Framework for the present research project (Schoja 2013)

The second objective 'Examine the factors which determines the consumer decision making process, their perception and expectation.' was answered both, from previous and recent research. The factors product quality and a convenient location determines the consumer decision making process the most (Mintel 2012). Though, in this research the most important aspects were product quality and a reasonable price. This findings were not properly consistent.

To investigate how customers define service quality was the third objective which were analysed from the findings in this research. Based on the conceptual framework, respondents perceive integrity, competence of staff and courtesy as most vital factors.

The last objective considered consumer attitude towards an existing problem, the tax avoidance of Starbucks. As there has been no previous research done on this issue the analysis focus the recent research only. Females recognise Starbucks' tax avoidance as more significant. Moreover 50% of customers who are aware of Starbucks' tax avoidance do not purchase Starbucks products anymore.

As discussed in the literature review an unsatisfied customer will spread they unhappiness with others by word of mouth (Heppel 2010). Similar to Heppel, Noel (2009) argue that dissatisfaction can lead to encourage to non-purchase through negative review. Even a boycott can be evoked by unsatisfied customers.

5.1 Conclusion for the Researcher

In result of this research benefits have been made to the researcher in direction of wider knowledge of consumer behaviour and improved following skills: Cognitive skills, problem solving and decision making, research and investigative skills, information and technology skills, numeracy and quantitative skills, communication and personal management skills.

6. Recommendations

As the findings show the importance of quality, companies should maintain and reinforce the level of product quality to satisfy customers in the first stage. This will lead to high performance and high revenue within the business.

Consumer also perceive staff competence as an essential aspect. Building on this fact companies ought to provide their employees further trainings for them to provide the best quality according to customer needs.

For Starbucks to satisfy the customers' which boycott Starbucks' products, qualitative interviews should be implemented to get in-depth information about their attitude and behaviour. Another important step is a press release about the current issue and modifications. This would show the customer's Starbucks' awareness and willingness for improvement.

References

Babones, S. (2012) *Research Paper and Publication: On corporate taxes, Britain follows U.S. lead* [online] available from <http://prijipati.library.usyd.edu.au/handle/2123/8853> [10 June 2013]

Bryman, A. and Bell, E. (2011) *Business Research Methods*, 3rd edn. New York: Oxford University Press Inc.

Collins, H. (2010) *Creative Research: The Theory and Practice of Research*, Lausanne: Ava Publishing SA

Collis, J. and Hussey, R. (2009) *Business Research*, 3rd edn. Hampshire: Palgrave Macmillian

Denscombe, M. (2007) *The Good Research Guide*, 3rd edn. Berkshire: Open University Press

Dibb, S. and Simkin, L. (2009) *Marketing Essentials*, Hampshire: Cengage Learning EMEA

Dul, J. and Hak, T. (2008) *Case Study: Methodology in Business Research*, Oxford: Elsevier Ltd

Easterby-Smith, M. Thorpe, R. and Jackson, P. (2011) *Management Research*, 3rd edn, London: SAGE Publications Ltd

Etisphire Institut (2013) 2013 *World's Most Ethical Companies* [online] available from <http://m1.ethisphere.com/wme2013/index.html> [10 May 2013]

Fetterman, D. (2010) *Ethnography, Step-by-Step*, 3rd edn. Thousand Oaks: Sage Publications, Inc.

Fitzmaurice, G. et al. (2011) *Applied Longitudinal Analysis*, 2nd edn. New Yersey: John Wiley & Sons, Inc.

Flick, U. (2011) I*ntroduction Research Methodology: A Beginner's Giude to Doing a Research Project*, London: SAGE Publications Ltd

Garmines, E. and Zeller, R. (1979) *Reliability and Validity Assessment*, Thousand Oaks: Sage Publications, Inc.

Gummersson, E. (1991) *Qualitative Methods in Management Research*, Newbury Park: Sage

Heppel, M. (2010) *5 Star Service*, 2nd edn. Harlow: Pearson Education Limited

Jobber, D. (2010) *Principles and Practice of Marketing*, 6th edn. Berkshire: McGraw-Hill Education

Johnston, R. Clark, G. and Shulver, M. (2012) *Service operations management*, 4th edn. Essex: Pearson Education Limited

Kothari, C. (2008) *Research Methodology*, 2nd edn. New Delhi: New Age International

Kotler, P. Amstrong, G. Harker, M. and Brennan, R. (2009) *Marketing: An Introduction*, Essex: Pearson Education Limited

Kumar, R. (2010) *Research Methodology: A step-by-step guide for beginners*, 3rd edn. London: SAGE Publications Ltd

MacDaniel, C. (1998) *Marketing Research Essentials*, 2nd edn. Salt Lake City: International Thomson Publishing

Metro (2013) *Tesco takes out full-page newspaper adverts to say sorry for horse meat burgers* [online] available from <<http://metro.co.uk/2013/01/17/tesco-takes-out-full-page-newspaper-adverts-to-say-sorry-for-horse-meat-burgers-3355674/> [10 June 2013]

Murphy, R. (2013) *Over Here and Undertaxed: Multinationals, Tax Avoidance and You*, London: Vintage Digital

Noel, H. (2009) *Consumer behaviour*, Lausanne: AVA Publishing SA

O'Leary, Z. (2004) *Guide to doing Research*, London: SAGE Publications Ltd

Oakshott, L. (2012) *Essential Quantitative Methods*, 5th edn. Hampshire: Palgrave Macmillian

Oliver, P. (2012) *Succeeding with your Literature Review*: A Handbook for Students, Berkshire: McGraw-Hill Education

Polonsky, M. and Valler, D. (2011) *Designing and Managing a Research Project*, London: SAGE Publications Ltd

Richey, R. and Klein, J.D. (2007) D*esign and Development Research: Methods, Strategies, and Issues*, New Jersey: Lawrence Erlbaum Associates, Inc. Publishers

Skiadas, C. (2009) *Quantitative and Qualitative Methods in Libraries: Theory and Applications*, Singapore: World Scientific Publishing Co Pte. Ltd

Starbucks (2013) *Our company* [online] available from <http://www.starbucks.co.uk/about-us/company-information> [02 May 2013]

Starbucks Coffee Company (2011) *Business Ethics and Compliance* [online] available from <http://www.starbucks.com/assets/eecd184d6d2141d58966319744393d1f.pdf> [10 May 2013]

Stevens, D. (2010) *Brilliant Customer Services*, 2nd edn. Harlow: Pearson Education Limited

Strauss, A. and Corbin, J. (1990) *Grounded Theory Methodology*: An Overview, CA: Sage

Appendices

Appendix 1 - Questionnaire for the primary research

Cover Letter:

Dear participant,

This questionnaire is a part of a research project to investigate the factors which influence consumer behaviour in the catering industry and will play an essential role for the evaluation for my business research project.

This research will be implemented in cooperation with Coventry University, London Campus, and the answers you provide will be used as the main dataset for my research project for my Bachelor degree in Global Marketing.

This questionnaire will require approximately 5 minutes to complete and your participation is important for me to obtain a better understanding of the topic. Nevertheless, your decision to take part is strictly voluntary and you are free to refuse at any time without justification.

All the information you provide in this questionnaire will be treated highly confidentially as the results will be used in summary form only. You will not be asked to include any personal details in the questionnaire. Additional, no identifying information will be shared. There are no risks associated with participating in this study

If you have any questions regarding the survey or would lik to get further information, please do not hesitate to contact me (schojav@culcuni.coventry.ac.uk).

Your participation is appreciated.

Kind regards

Viktoria Schoja

1. What is your gender? (Compulsory question)

- ○ Male
- ○ Female

2. What is your age? (Compulsory question)

- ○ Under 16
- ○ 16 to 24
- ○ 25 to 34
- ○ 35 to 49
- ○ 50 or older

3. Where do you currently live? (Compulsory question)

- ○ London
- ○ Other cities in UK
- ○ Other cities outside UK

4 What does service quality mean to you? Please rank each one of the factors below in order of importance. (Compulsory question)

1 stands for least important and 6 stands for most important.

	1	2	3	4	5	6
Availability (service)	○	○	○	○	○	○
Comfort (facilities)	○	○	○	○	○	○
Competence (staff)	○	○	○	○	○	○
Courtesy (politeness, respect)	○	○	○	○	○	○
Flexibility (willingness to meet customer needs)	○	○	○	○	○	○
Integrity (honesty and trustworthiness with which customer are treated by the organisation)	○	○	○	○	○	○
Responsiveness (speed of service delivery)	○	○	○	○	○	○
Knowing the customer (to be able to provide the best service)	○	○	○	○	○	○
Appearance of personnel	○	○	○	○	○	○

5 How important are the following factors for you, when choosing a coffee/tea shop? (Compulsory question)

1 stands for least important and 6 stands for most important.

	1	2	3	4	5	6
Price (do you prefer lower prices?)	○	○	○	○	○	○
Product quality (do you prefer good quality?)	○	○	○	○	○	○
Shop-access (do you prefer shops which you can access and find easily	○	○	○	○	○	○
Sustainability (is the company sustainable?)	○	○	○	○	○	○
Taxes (is the company paying their taxes?)	○	○	○	○	○	○
Fair trade (is the company provides fair trade products?)	○	○	○	○	○	○
Staff care (is it important how the company treats their staff?)	○	○	○	○	○	○

6 Have you heard of Starbucks' tax avoidance at the end of 2012? (Compulsory question)

○ Yes
○ No

7 If yes, what was the first medium?

○ Newspaper
○ Television
○ Facebook
○ Twitter
○ Work/School/University
○ Friends
○ Online News
○ Other web channels (specify which)

8 If yes, did you tend to avoid buying Starbucks products after the tax avoidance was published?

○ Yes
○ No

9 Please name 5 (or as many as you can) coffee/tea chains you associate with hot drinks (Compulsory question)

Thank you for taking part. You can now close your browser.

Appendix 2 - Findings from the primary research

Factors which influnce consumer behaviour in the catering industry.

Page 1, Question 1: What is your gender? (Compulsory question)
161 Participant

Male	74
Female	87

Page 1, Question 2: What is your age? (Compulsory question)
161 Participant

Under 16	3
16 to 24	77
25 to 34	59
35 to 49	19
50 or older	3

Page 1, Question 3: Where do you currently live? (Compulsory question)
161 Participant

London	137
Other cities in UK	12
Other cities outside UK	12

Page 2, Question 4: What does service quality mean to you? Please rank each one of the factors below in order of importance. (Compulsory question)
1 stands for least important and 6 stands for most important.
161 Participant

	1	2	3	4	5	6
Availability (service)	3	6	25	47	44	36
Comfort (facilities)	0	2	14	61	64	20
Competence (staff)	1	1	12	42	63	42
Courtesy (politeness, respect)	1	0	11	41	58	50
Flexibility (willingness to meet customer needs)	0	3	15	50	62	31
Integrity (honesty and trustworthiness with which customer are treated by the organisation)	2	3	15	37	50	54
Responsiveness (speed of service delivery)	1	3	21	44	55	37
Knowing the customer (to be able to provide the best service)	2	2	23	49	55	30
Appearance of personnel	4	14	29	54	43	17

Page 2, Question 5: How important are the following factors for you, when choosing a coffee/tea shop? (Compulsory question)
1 stands for least important and 6 stands for most important.
161 Participant

	1	2	3	4	5	6
Price (do you prefer lower prices?)	2	5	32	46	31	45
Product quality (do you prefer good quality?)	1	1	4	21	45	89
Shop-access (do you prefer shops which you can access and find easily	4	11	20	55	50	21
Sustainability (is the company sustainable?)	7	16	27	54	42	15
Taxes (is the company paying their taxes?)	19	10	25	51	36	20
Fair trade (is the company provides fair trade products?)	7	12	31	52	42	17
Staff care (is it important how the company treats their staff?)	7	5	14	49	53	33

Page 3, Question 6: Have you heard of Starbucks' tax avoidance at the end of 2012? (Compulsory question)
161 Participant

Yes	111
No	50

Page 3, Question 7: If yes, what was the first medium?
112 Participant

Newspaper	51	
Television	13	
Facebook	10	
Twitter	2	
Work/School/University	12	
Friends	5	
Online News	16	
Other web channels (specify which)	3	☐ radio ☐ yahoo ☐ the sun online

Page 3, Question 8: If yes, did you tend to avoid buying Starbucks products after the tax avoidance was published?
118 Participant

Yes	55
No	63

Page 4, Question 9: Please name 5 (or as many as you can) coffee/tea chains you associate with hot drinks (Compulsory question)
161 Participant

A detailed list can be provided upon request

Appendix 3 – Ethics List

Low Risk Research Ethics Approval Checklist

Applicant Details

Viktoria Schoja	schojav@culcuni.coventry.ac.uk
Global Marketing Top-Up	21/06/2013
308LON – Work-based project	What factors play the greatest role in determining consumer behaviour in the catering industry: A case study of Starbucks, United kingdom

Project Details

- The purpose of this research is to study consumer behaviour within the catering industry and to investigate the factors which determine customer consumption preferences as well as the main buying criteria for customers towards a hot drinks company. Research Objectives:

1. Investigate the determinants which affect the consumer behaviour and satisfaction and develop a conceptual framework for the research project based on previous studies.
2. Examine the factors which determines the consumer decision making process, their perception and expectation.
3. Explore how customers define service quality.
4. Observe consumer attitude towards an existing problem: tax avoidance of Starbucks.

- The questionnaire was spread online by using social media as a prime source

Participants in your research

1.	Will the project involve human participants?	Yes

If you answered **Yes** to this questions, this may not be a low risk project.

- If you are a student, please discuss your project with your Supervisor.
- If you are a member of staff, please discuss your project with your Faculty Research Ethics Leader or use the Medium to High Risk Ethical Approval or NHS or Medical Approval Routes.

Risk to Participants

#	Question		
2.	Will the project involve human patients/clients, health professionals, and/or patient (client) data and/or health professional data?		No
3.	Will any invasive physical procedure, including collecting tissue or other samples, be used in the research?		No
4.	Is there a risk of physical discomfort to those taking part?		No
5.	Is there a risk of psychological or emotional distress to those taking part?		No
6.	Is there a risk of challenging the deeply held beliefs of those taking part?		No
7.	Is there a risk that previous, current or proposed criminal or illegal acts will be revealed by those taking part?		No
8.	Will the project involve giving any form of professional, medical or legal advice, either directly or indirectly to those taking part?		No

If you answered **Yes** to **any** of these questions, this may **not** be a low risk project.

- If you are a student, please discuss your project with your Supervisor.
- If you are a member of staff, please discuss your project with your Faculty Research Ethics Leader or use the Medium to High Risk Ethical Approval or NHS or Medical Approval Routes.

Risk to Researcher

9. Will this project put you or others at risk of physical harm, injury or death?		No
10. Will project put you or others at risk of abduction, physical, mental or sexual abuse?		No
11. Will this project involve participating in acts that may cause psychological or emotional distress to you or to others?		No
12. Will this project involve observing acts which may cause psychological or emotional distress to you or to others?		No
13. Will this project involve reading about, listening to or viewing materials that may cause psychological or emotional distress to you or to others?		No
14. Will this project involve you disclosing personal data to the participants other than your name and the University as your contact and e-mail address?	Yes	
15. Will this project involve you in unsupervised private discussion with people who are not already known to you?		No
16. Will this project potentially place you in the situation where you may receive unwelcome media attention?		No
17. Could the topic or results of this project be seen as illegal or attract the attention of the security services or other agencies?		No
18. Could the topic or results of this project be viewed as controversial by anyone?		No

If you answered **Yes** to **any** of these questions, this is not a low risk project. Please:

- If you are a student, discuss your project with your Supervisor.
- If you are a member of staff, discuss your project with your Faculty Research Ethics Leader or use the Medium to High Risk Ethical Approval route.

Informed Consent of the Participant

19. Are any of the participants under the age of 18?	Yes	
20. Are any of the participants unable mentally or physically to give consent?		No
21. Do you intend to observe the activities of individuals or groups without their knowledge and/or informed consent from each participant (or from his or her parent or guardian)?		No

If you answered **Yes** to **any** of these questions, this may not be a low risk project. Please:

- If you are a student, discuss your project with your Supervisor.
- If you are a member of staff, discuss your project with your Faculty Research Ethics Leader or use the Medium to High Risk Ethical Approval route.

Participant Confidentiality and Data Protection

22. Will the project involve collecting data and information from human participants who will be identifiable in the final report?		No
23. Will information not already in the public domain about specific individuals or institutions be identifiable through data published or otherwise made available?		No
24. Do you intend to record, photograph or film individuals or groups without their knowledge or informed consent?		No
25. Do you intend to use the confidential information, knowledge or trade secrets gathered for any purpose other than this research project?		No

If you answered **Yes** to **any** of these questions, this may not be a low risk project:
- If you are a student, discuss your project with your Supervisor.
- If you are a member of staff, discuss your project with your Faculty Research Ethics Leader or use the Medium to High Risk Ethical Approval or NHS or Medical Approval routes.

Gatekeeper Risk

26. Will this project involve collecting data outside University buildings?	Yes	
27. Do you intend to collect data in shopping centres or other public places?		No
28. Do you intend to gather data within nurseries, schools or colleges?		No
29. Do you intend to gather data within National Health Service premises?		No

If you answered **Yes** to **any** of these questions, this is not a low risk project. Please:
- If you are a student, discuss your project with your Supervisor.
- If you are a member of staff, discuss your project with your Faculty Research Ethics Leader or use the Medium to High Risk Ethical Approval or NHS or Medical Approval routes.

Other Ethical Issues

30. Is there any other risk or issue not covered above that may pose a risk to you or any of the participants?		No
31. Will any activity associated with this project put you or the participants at an ethical, moral or legal risk?		No

If you answered **Yes** to these questions, this may not be a low risk project. Please:
- If you are a student, discuss your project with your Supervisor.
- If you are a member of staff, discuss your project with your Faculty Research Ethics Leader.

Principal Investigator Certification

If you answered **No** to all of the above questions, then you have described a low risk project. Please complete the following declaration to certify your project and keep a copy for your record as you may be asked for this at any time.

Agreed restrictions to project to allow Principal Investigator Certification

Please identify any restrictions to the project, agreed with your Supervisor or Faculty Research Ethics Leader to allow you to sign the Principal Investigator Certification declaration.

Principal Investigator's Declaration

Please ensure that you:

- Tick all the boxes below and sign this checklist.
- Students must get their Supervisor to countersign this declaration.

I believe that this project **does not require research ethics approval**. I have completed the checklist and kept a copy for my own records. I realise I may be asked to provide a copy of this checklist at any time.	
I confirm that I have answered all relevant questions in this checklist honestly.	
I confirm that I will carry out the project in the ways described in this checklist. I will immediately suspend research and request a new ethical approval if the project subsequently changes the information I have given in this checklist.	

Signatures

If you or your supervisor do not have electronic signatures, please type your name in the signature space. An email sent from the Supervisor's University inbox will be accepted as having been signed electronically.

Principal Investigator

Signed ....(Principal Investigator or Student)

Date ....

Students storing this checklist electronically must append to it an email from your Supervisor confirming that they are prepared to make the declaration above and to countersign this checklist. This email will be taken as an electronic countersignature.

Student's Supervisor

Countersigned..(Supervisor)

Date ....

I have read this checklist and confirm that it covers all the ethical issues raised by this project fully and frankly. I also confirm that these issues have been discussed with the student and will continue to be reviewed in the course of supervision.